Ladybirds

CLAIRE LLEWELLYN • BARRIE WATTS

W

FRANKLIN WATTS
LONDON•SYDNEY

This edition 2003

Franklin Watts
96 Leonard Street
London
EC2A 4XD

Franklin Watts Australia
45–51 Huntley Street
Alexandria
NSW 2015

Series editor: Rachel Cooke
Editor: Rosalind Beckman
Series designer: Jason Anscomb
Designer: Joelle Wheelwright
Illustrator: David Burroughs

A CIP catalogue record is available
from the British Library.
Dewey Classification 595.76

ISBN 0 7496 5206 3

Printed in Hong Kong/China

Contents

What are ladybirds? 6–7

A ladybird's food 8–9

On the wing 10–11

Laying eggs 12–13

Life as a larva 14–15

Becoming an adult 16–17

Staying alive 18–19

In a swarm 20–21

A winter sleep 22–23

The gardener's friend 24–25

Ladybird life! 26–27

Glossary 28

Index 29

What are ladybirds?

Ladybirds are small, round, brightly-coloured beetles. Most of them are red or yellow with black spots, but some are brown or have different colour spots, and a few have no spots at all.

▲ *A 22-spot ladybird*

▲ *A 7-spot ladybird*

▲ *A 14-spot ladybird*

Each kind of ladybird has its own pattern of spots.

Ladybirds belong to the insect family. Like all insects, they have three parts to their body: the head, the thorax and the abdomen.

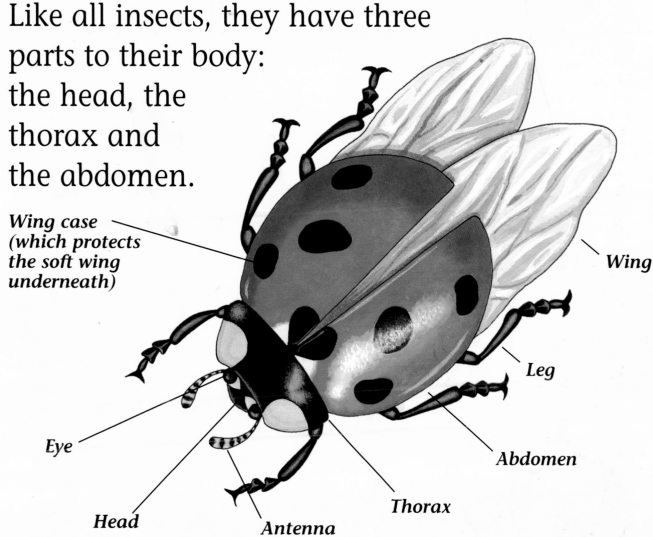

Wing case (which protects the soft wing underneath)

Wing

Eye

Leg

Abdomen

Head

Antenna

Thorax

Ladybirds have three pairs of legs. All the parts of the body are covered in a tough case called the exoskeleton.

A ladybird uses its antennae to touch, taste and smell things, and to pick up movements in the air.

A ladybird's food

Ladybirds are always hungry. They feed mostly on aphids. These are the green, black or white insects you see on roses and other plants.

▲

Aphids smother buds and stems and feed on the sweet juice inside.

Aphids are easy to catch because they move very slowly. They have soft, plump bodies, which are full of the juice they suck out of plants.

Like many beetles, ladybirds have strong jaws that are good at biting and chewing. They make short work of aphids and other tiny creatures.

A ladybird eats about 100 aphids a day.

On the wing

Ladybirds spend most of their time crawling around on the ground, but they can fly when they need to. They fly to escape from danger, or to look further afield for food.

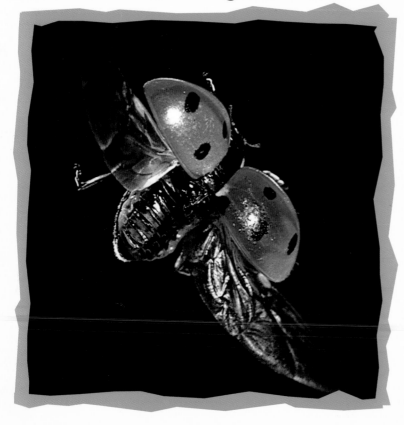

Ladybirds have two pairs of wings. The front pair are hard wing cases. These protect the back pair, which are folded out of sight underneath when not in use.

A ladybird prepares for flight.

❶ *Before take-off, a ladybird crawls to the top of a stem.* ▶

◀ **❷** *It opens its hard wing cases.*

❸ *It unfolds its delicate flying wings and beats them up and down.* ▶

◀ **❹** *Soon the wings beat so quickly that they lift the ladybird into the air.*

Laying eggs

Like many insects, a ladybird goes through four different stages as it grows called its life cycle. The first stage of its life cycle is an egg on a plant.

❶ *Male and female ladybirds mate in the warm days of spring and summer.*

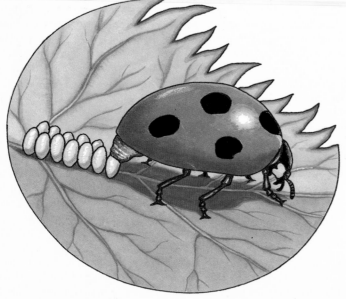

❷ *About a week later, the female lays her eggs on a plant where there are plenty of aphids.*

About a week after they are laid, the eggs change colour. They are ready to hatch. The thin shells begin to split, and wriggly creatures called larvae crawl out. The larva is the second stage of a ladybird's life cycle.

❸ *The tiny yellow eggs stand up like skittles. There are about 20–30 eggs in a batch.*

❹ *All the eggs hatch at the same time. The tiny larvae twist and turn until they can wriggle free of the shell.*

▼

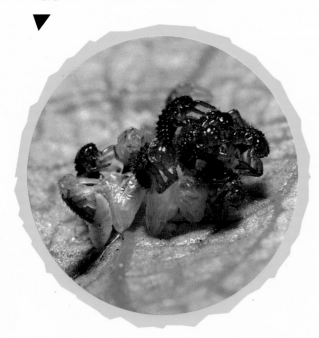

❺ *Once the larvae have hatched, their first meal is the egg shell.*

▲

Life as a larva

A ladybird larva looks nothing like its parents. It has a long, thin body made up of segments, which are covered with tiny bristles. It has three pairs of legs like an adult ladybird, but it has no wings and cannot fly.

Ladybird larvae feed on aphids, just as their parents do. They eat so many that they grow very quickly, and are soon too big for their skin. The old skin splits open and the larva wriggles out, wearing a new skin with room to grow.

This larva is hunting for food. It eats about 30 aphids every day.

Becoming an adult

About three weeks after hatching from its egg, a larva is fully grown. It stops feeding and glues itself to a plant. Now it will become a pupa. This is the third stage in a ladybird's life cycle.

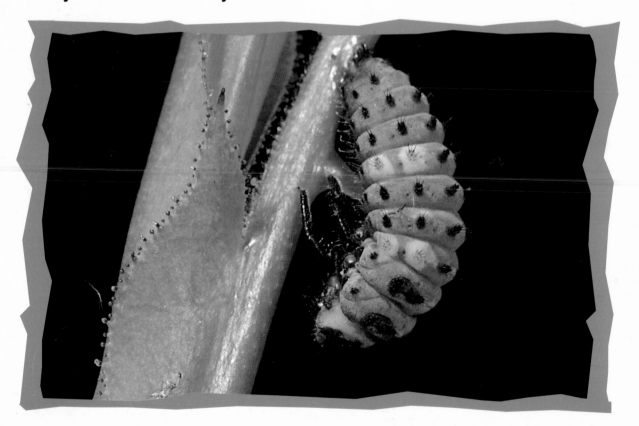

A larva attaches itself to a plant before becoming a pupa.

From pupa to ladybird

❶ The larva has shed its skin for the last time and is turning into a pupa. Inside the pupa, the insect's body is now beginning to change.

❷ About a week later, the pupa splits open and an adult ladybird crawls out.

❸ A ladybird's wing cases are yellow at first. They take 24 hours to turn red and for the spots to appear.

Staying alive

Ladybirds have a clever way of staying alive – they smell and taste very bad. Most animals that try to eat them usually spit them out.

It is a lesson the animal never forgets. When it next sees beetles with bright-red wing cases, it leaves them well alone!

A ladybird's spots and bright colours are a warning that it tastes very bad.

When a ladybird is frightened, a bitter, yellow juice oozes out of its legs. This often puts the enemy off.

◄ *Ladybirds still have some enemies. This ladybird is being attacked by a shieldbug.*

If a ladybird is attacked, it defends itself by making a nasty-tasting poison and giving a painful bite. It may even roll over and pretend to be dead.

In a swarm

Ladybirds sometimes gather in huge groups called swarms and fly off somewhere new. They do this when there are too many of them in one place and food is growing short. Spreading out helps them to survive.

A swarm of ladybirds spreads out to look for food.

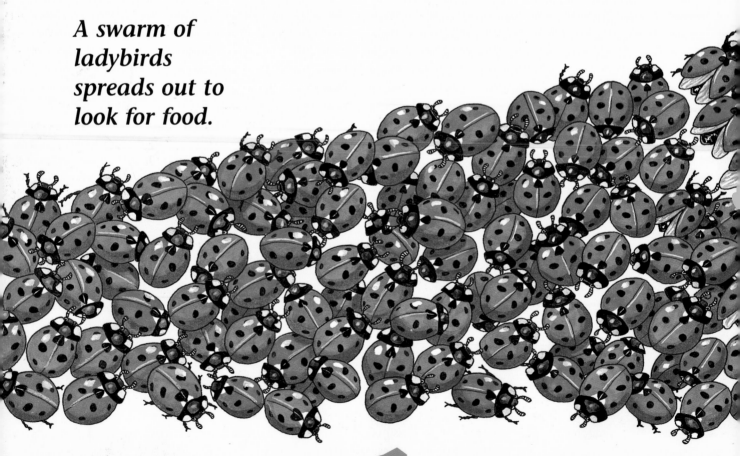

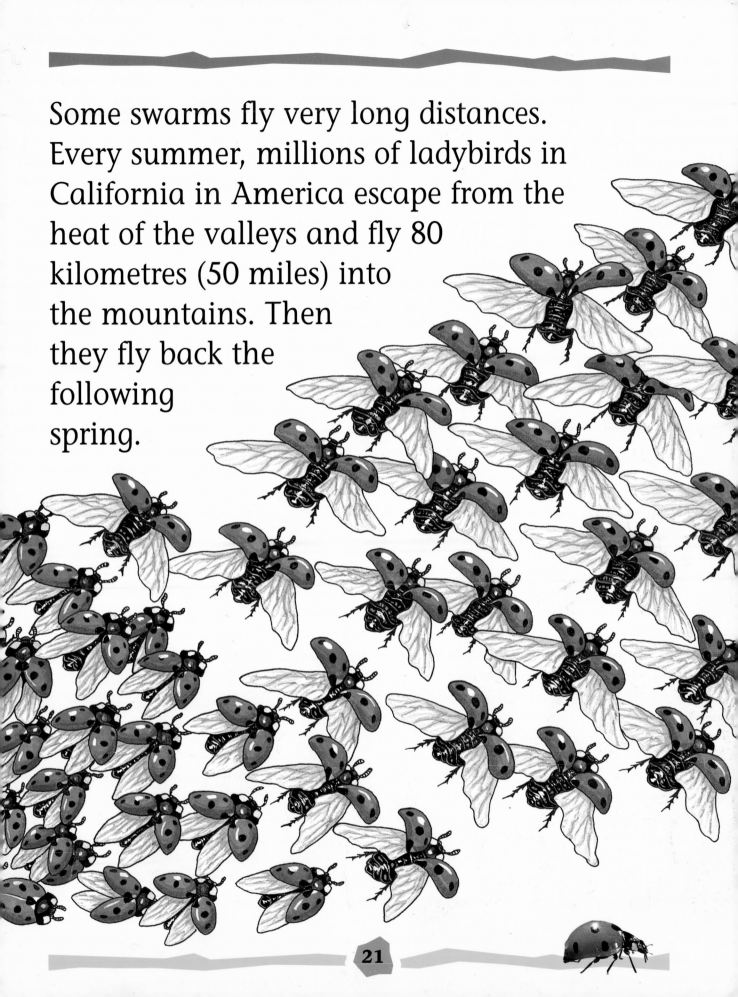

Some swarms fly very long distances.
Every summer, millions of ladybirds in
California in America escape from the
heat of the valleys and fly 80
kilometres (50 miles) into
the mountains. Then
they fly back the
following
spring.

A winter sleep

Ladybirds that develop during the late summer hibernate in winter. The weather is too cold and there are no aphids to eat. They huddle under the bark of a tree or find their way into attics and sheds.

Some kinds of ladybirds spend the winter in the same places year after year.

Ladybird hibernating in the bark of a tree during the winter.

Sometimes millions of ladybirds squeeze together and hibernate under the snow. Their bodies contain a special chemical that stops them freezing to death.

When the snow melts in spring, they fly off to mate and look for food.

A blanket of snow protects ladybirds from the cold winter air.

The gardener's friend

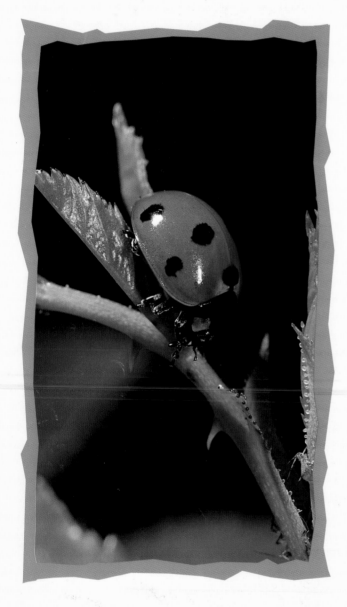

Ladybirds are a great help to gardeners and farmers. They feed on the pests that spoil plants and crops, so growers do not need chemicals to protect their crops. This is good for the food that we eat and good for the soil, too.

Ladybirds are a good way of getting rid of pests, without using chemical sprays.

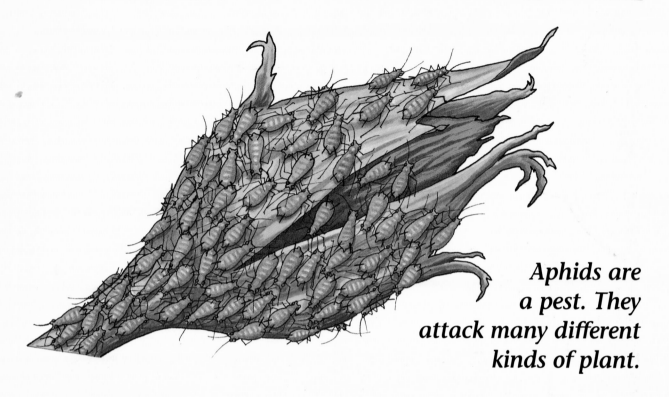

Aphids are a pest. They attack many different kinds of plant.

In some parts of the world, farmers buy ladybirds and larvae to spread around their fields. They hope that the insects will protect their plants and help them to harvest extra crops.

Some growers buy ladybirds to protect their plants.

Ladybird life!

It takes a ladybird about half an hour to crawl out of its pupa. It flies off after an hour.

Ladybirds beat their wings about 75–90 times a second.

Ladybird larvae are hungry when they hatch. If they cannot find aphids, they eat one another!

Some kinds of ladybird feed on plants. A few eat food crops and are real pests.

"Ladybird, ladybird, fly away home. Your house is on fire and your children all gone." People said this rhyme long ago after the harvest, when farmers set fire to their fields.

In folk medicine, ladybirds are thought to be a cure for toothache, measles and tummy ache.

There are over 4,000 different kinds of ladybird.

In America, ladybirds are known as ladybugs.

A female ladybird lays about 400 eggs in her lifetime.

The life cycle of a ladybird only takes 4 weeks. Ladybirds that develop in May can be great-grandparents by August!

Glossary

Abdomen   The last of the three parts of an insect's body.

Antenna   One of the two feelers on a ladybird's head. (Plural: antennae)

Beetles   A group of insects that have hard wing cases and can usually fly.

Exoskeleton   The hard outer coat that protects the body of insects and other small animals.

Larva   The young stage of an insect after it hatches out of an egg. (Plural: larvae)

Life cycle   All the different stages that an animal goes through in life, until it has its own young.

Pupa   The stage in an insect's life when it changes from a larva to an adult. (Plural: pupae)

Thorax   The middle part of an insect's body, in between the head and the abdomen.

Index

abdomen 7
antenna 7
aphids 8, 9, 12, 14, 15, 22, 25

beetles 6, 9, 18, 24
bristles 14

eggs 12, 13, 16
enemies 19
exoskeleton, 7

food 8, 9, 20
flying 10, 11, 20, 21, 23

hatching 13, 16
head 7
hibernation 22, 23

insects 7, 8

jaws 9

larva 13, 14, 15, 16, 17, 25
legs 7, 14
life cycle 12, 13

mating 12

pests 24
pupa 16, 17

segments 14
shieldbug 19
skin 14, 16
spots 6, 17, 18
staying alive 18, 19
swarm 20, 21

thorax 7

wings 7, 10, 11, 14
wing cases 7, 10, 11, 17, 18